Mr. Goo Goes Food Tripping: Famous Food and Delicacies in South America

BABY PROFESSOR
EDUCATION KIDS

In South America, people's normal food was a lot like what you know as Mexican food. People wrapped flat corn tortillas around refried beans, tomato and avocadoes, and added fish, turkey, and chili peppers for flavor.

Hot Tamales

Lucuma Cake

Causa

Staple latino
sides, manioc,
rice, plantains,
and black beans

Grilled chicken served with potato salad, salsa and black eyed pea salad

Beef Tacos

Tasty Taco sandwich

South American people also ate tamales, cooked in corn husks, and tortillas made with turkey eggs. Popcorn was popular in South America.

South American women freeze-dried the potatoes so they would keep all winter, and used them to make stews and soups spiced with chili peppers. People also ate a lot of corn.

Shrimp ceviche

Mexican chicken fajitas

Lomo Saltado

Fried slices of the
ripe plantain

Boiled crawfish
clayfish

Bolivian Saltena